JACOB EL HANANI

JACOB EL HANANI

LINESCAPE: FOUR DECADES

ACQUAVELLA

This publication accompanies the exhibition

JACOB EL HANANI
LINESCAPE: FOUR DECADES

ON VIEW
October 2–November 17, 2017

Acquavella Galleries
18 East Seventy-Ninth Street
New York, NY 10075

Library of Congress Control Number 2017953243

ISBN 978-0-9981156-3-4

DESIGN
HvADesign, NY

PRINT
Phoenix Lithographing, Philadelphia, PA

COVER (FRONT)
Alhambra, 2016 (DETAIL)
Ink on paper
25 $^7/_8$ x 25 $^3/_4$ inches (65.7 x 65.4 cm)

COVER (BACK)
Cloud Linescape, 2014 (DETAIL)
Ink on gessoed canvas
15 $^1/_8$ x 15 $^1/_4$ inches (38.4 x 38.7 cm)

FRONTISPIECE
Cross-Hatching Linescape, 2016 (DETAIL)
Ink on gessoed canvas
15 $^1/_8$ x 15 $^1/_8$ inches (38.4 x 38.4 cm)

PAGE 6
Circle-NOF, 2006 (DETAIL)
Ink on paper
15 x 17 inches (38.1 x 43.2 cm)

PAGE 8
Gray Gauze, 2016 (DETAIL)
Ink on paper
25 $^7/_8$ x 26 inches (65.7 x 66 cm)

Table of Contents

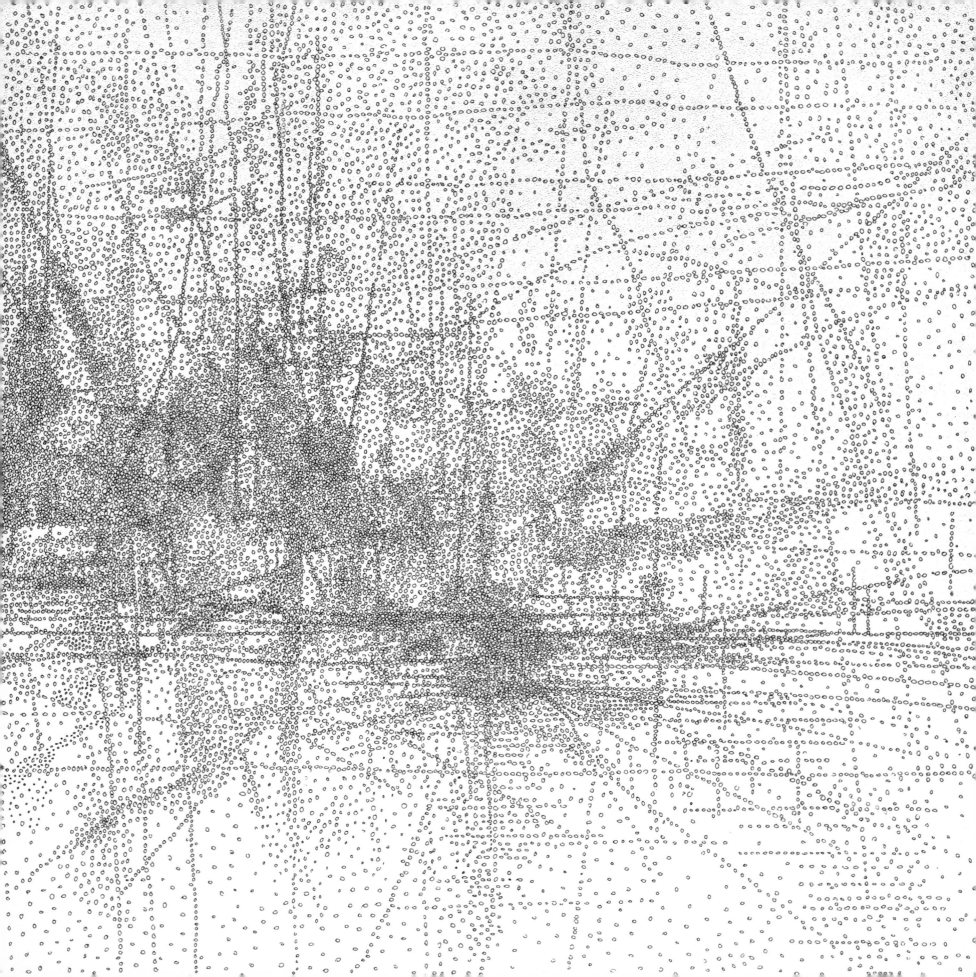

JACOB EL HANANI

ELEANOR ACQUAVELLA

WE ARE DELIGHTED TO PRESENT our second exhibition of Jacob El Hanani's work, a retrospective of four decades of the artist's drawings on canvas and paper. Over thirty works will be on view, the majority of which are being exhibited for the first time.

Since he moved to New York in the early 1970s, Jacob has been committed to his exacting process, creating meticulously detailed, all-over drawings with thousands of microscopic marks in pen. From a distance, his drawings appear to be shimmering, abstract fields; only at close range does the viewer appreciate their painstakingly detailed surfaces. Working without a magnifying glass in ten-minute stints— the artist has to take breaks to rest his eyes—these drawings take months or even years to complete, speaking to the passage of time and the limits of human endurance. In the fast-paced tempo of today's world, the deliberate slowness of Jacob's work strikes a counterpoint; his images aren't immediately understandable and require more than a few seconds to grasp in their complexity.

While our first exhibition focused on works on paper, this show also includes over a dozen works on canvas, a medium the artist frequently worked in during the 1970s and has returned to in recent years. Applying ink with a quill to his gessoed surfaces, these works demand the same unrelenting precision as his works on paper, though often at a larger scale.

The exhibition takes its title from Jacob's "linescape" series, which represents the artist's interpretation of the theme of landscape. Though at first these works appear abstract and indebted to the aesthetic rigors of minimalism, they also subtly evoke the history of landscape painting. Inspired by Turner's dramatic sense of light and atmosphere, several of the works are named for the British master, while others look to Mondrian's linear grids to achieve a feeling of urban landscape. For the artist, these works represent a liberation from his highly detailed and rigidly structured earlier series.

For their help in making this exhibition possible, we would like to warmly thank Raphael Rubinstein for his insightful essay; the team at the gallery including Emily Crowley, Jean Edmonson, Garth Szwed, Eric Theriault, Kim Vick, and Devon Vogt; and Keith Harrington at Phoenix Lithographing and Henk van Assen for their work in producing this catalogue. Above all, our gratitude goes to the artist for making these beautiful works and helping with the many facets of the exhibition.

JACOB EL HANANI
INFINITE TERRITORIES

RAPHAEL RUBINSTEIN

IN A 1964 LECTURE AT THE LEO BAECK INSTITUTE in New York, the great scholar of Jewish mysticism Gershom Scholem memorialized his friendship with Walter Benjamin, then dead for nearly a quarter century. At the time Benjamin was still little known in the English-speaking world though, as Scholem pointed out to his audience, his star had steadily been rising in Germany since the posthumous publication of a volume of his writings in 1955. Of course, Benjamin's impact was soon to spread far and wide as his prescient essay "The Work of Art in the Age of Mechanical Reproduction" became required reading for every art student and his Arcades Project furnished countless writers and artists with tools for making critical assessments of modernity. Desirous to convey to a New York audience both the historical significance of his vanished friend, and his great originality and remarkable personality, Scholem enriched his lecture with glimpses of Benjamin's abiding passions. Prominent among these was a penchant for the diminutive. What must be understood about Benjamin, Scholem explained, was that "to create, or discover, perfection on the small and very small scale was one of his strongest urges," an urge that could be seen in Benjamin's "never-realized ambition to get a hundred lines onto an ordinary sheet of paper" and his penchant for miniature texts.[1] (A friend of Benjamin's, Jean Selz, once recalled how Benjamin "never found a pen that was fine enough" for the minute script he desired so that he was compelled "to write with the nib upside down."[2]) [FIG. 1 NEXT PAGE] As evidence of this mania for miniatures, Scholem recalled a long-ago encounter with Benjamin: "In August 1927, he dragged me to the Musée Cluny in Paris, where in a collection of Jewish ritual objects, he showed me with true rapture two grains of wheat on which a kindred soul had inscribed the complete Shema Israel."[3]

Given the fact that Scholem argues throughout the lecture for the deeply Jewish nature of Benjamin's thinking and writing, it's surprising that he doesn't associate Benjamin's love of tiny writing with the Jewish tradition of micrography. Instead, he links it with Benjamin's quest, crucial for his aphoristic book *One-Way Street*, "to present in the briefest literary utterance something complete in itself."[4]

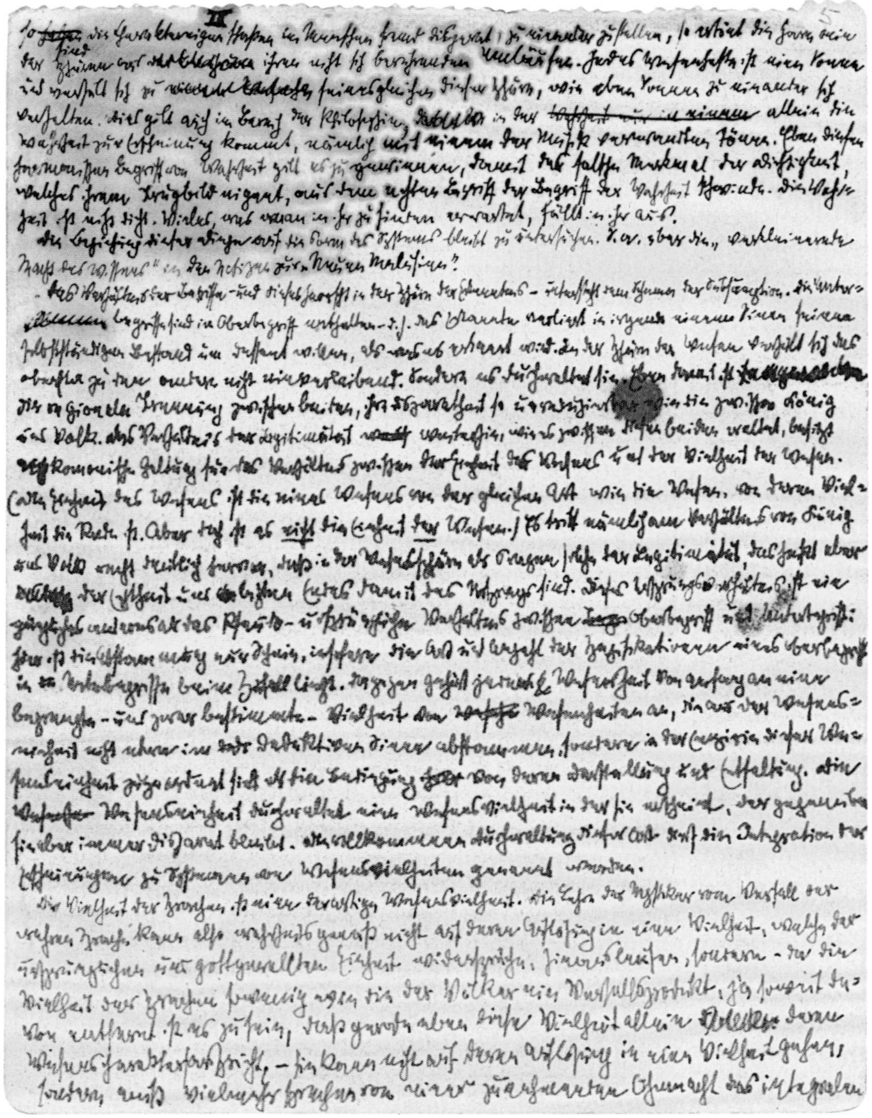

FIG. 1
Manuscript page from Walter Benjamin,
Language and Logic II, 1921
Akademie der Künste, Berlin,
Walter Benjamin Archiv

At first glance, Jacob El Hanani's micrographic ink drawings seem to partake of the same spirit as Benjamin's hyper-condensed notes and manuscripts. Clearly both men appreciate "perfection on the small and very small scale." It's even easy to imagine El Hanani, who studied in Paris around 1970, dragging you to see those wheat grains incised with Judaism's central prayer on the Rue des Écoles. (I wonder, are they still on display at the Musée Cluny today)? But there are also ways in which Benjamin and El Hanani diverge, even radically, in their approach to micro-writing.[5]

If Benjamin hoped to "present in the briefest literary utterance something complete in itself," El Hanani's ambition as an artist is far from any such brevity, nor does he share Benjamin's love of the fragmentary. Instead, his domain is the epic, the infinite, and the endless, a kind of oceanic sublime. A casual viewer of El Hanani's work might be forgiven for not immediately noticing this dimension of his art. With his extreme economy of means—nothing more than a pen or quill, some black ink and a sheet of white paper or, on occasion, canvas—and the generally small size of his drawings, El Hanani can give the impression of being a reductive artist, a minimal miniaturist, but as soon as one begins to linger in front of any one of his drawings (and prolonged viewing is the only way to apprehend them), their expansiveness and vast scale become impossible to avoid. The greater the number of miniscule marks that El Hanani can fit into a square inch, the larger that space becomes. It's as if he uses his pen like a scalpel, with each stroke opening a new fissure in space, separating it the way one might separate the fibers in a ball of cotton. In his drawings a postage-stamp area can begin to feel like a glimpse into infinitude.

Metaphysics as well as physics have long been concerned with locating more things, be they angels or subatomic particles, into ever-smaller spaces, thus edging closer to infinity, and there are fascinating ways in which El Hanani engages both of these realms. However, his art is grounded in reality, analog reality. The fact that he can go no further than the limits of his eyesight and stamina, the manual ability of his drawing hand and the capacities of his tools and materials, means that his art has little to do with the miniaturization that is so crucial to current technology. His drawings are not some stopping point on the road to nanotechnology; they have nothing to do with Moore's Law.[6] Paradoxically, these artworks that seem to defy the normal limits of the human hand and eye, pushing artist and viewer to perceptual extremes, may actually act as reminders of our finitude, our ineluctable corporeality, rather than its opposite.

Curiously, there is another 20th-century German-speaking author who was also deeply invested in miniature scripts: Robert Walser (1878-1956). [FIG. 2] A Swiss-born writer who gained a modicum of fame as a novelist and feuilletonist in the 1910s and 1920s—Benjamin and Kafka were among his appreciative readers—Walser suffered from schizophrenia and spent the last 27 years of his life confined to asylums. After his death a trove of his manuscripts was discovered featuring such tiny writing that it took decades for them to be deciphered. These so-called microscripts were written in pencil on the backs of business cards, tear-off calendar pages and assorted printed ephemera. In her introduction to a volume devoted to the microscripts, translator Susan Bernofsky describes Walser's "pencil system": "By filling up page after page with crabbed writing so small it defied legibility, he broke radically from the aesthetic ideal of the elegantly inscribed page he had pursued for so long. In this completely new sort of aesthetic, the shape of an individual letter was no longer in danger of not passing muster—single letters in his new handwriting were often not even visible! Lower-case *n*'s began to resemble *e*'s, indistinguishable verti-cal ticks or scratches."[7] By his own account, Walser turned to micro-writing to avoid the chronic hand cramp and writer's block he suffered when writing with ink; writing at a minute

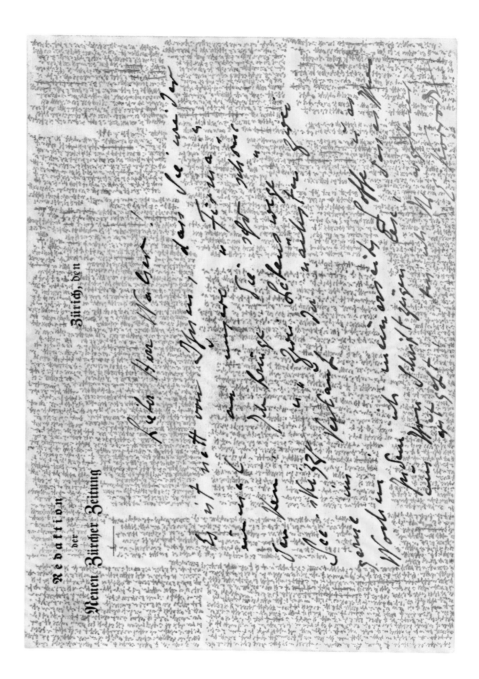

FIG. 2
Excerpt of Robert Walser, *Microscript #9*

scale in pencil let him work "more dreamily, peacefully, cozily, contemplatively."[8] As Bernofsky observes, Walser experienced a creative freedom when not even he could read what he was writing, thus "relieving him of the burden of being always, as he wrote, in the spotlight of his own critical judgment."[9]

While the procedures followed by El Hanani—who always sees clearly the marks he is making—are far removed from Walser's intentionally unreadable manuscripts, both artist and writer are drawn to the frontiers of their respective mediums. For Walser, writing, at least the kind of writing he wants to accomplish, appears to be possible only at the verge of illegibility, while for El Hanani, drawing can only flourish at the edge of visibility, and at the extreme precision of the human hand.

Instantly, having situated El Hanani's drawings "at the edge of visibility" I realize that it is only at the close-up, please-hand-me-a-magnifying-glass level that his work flirts with invisibility—seen in their entirety his drawings are perfectly visible, if only as fields of gray, as mottled, undulating planes. In an important essay on El Hanani's work, the late Arthur Danto elucidates this double aspect of the drawings, what he calls their "two foci" (micrographic characters and the "abstract pattern") and how these two methods of viewing mutually determine each other: "The micrographic images are drawn in part in order that the abstract pattern fully emerge in the end, so it serves as a guide to the way the micrographic array is constructed."[10]

When we find artists or writers venturing to such extremes our curiosity about their motivations and influences, their creative journey, is enhanced. How is it, we ask ourselves in front of El Hanani's work, that an artist has devoted his career to making art that is so difficult to see, art that seems

FIG. 3
Jacob El Hanani, at right, with his brother Daniel, c. 1951–52, in Casablanca. Photograph by their father, Ruben Elhyani.

to turn away from all that we usually seek out in visual art (riveting compositions, chromatic pleasure, spatial illusion), at least in Western traditions? While no important artist is ever simply the sum of his or her influences, nor containable within a narrative of development, it might be helpful to look at El Hanani's history, at the changing contexts of his art-making.

Born in Casablanca in 1947, El Hanani spent the first six and a half years of his life as part of Morocco's vibrant Jewish community, which could trace its origins back thousands of years. Like most Jewish communities around the Mediterranean, Morocco experienced an influx of refugees after the expulsion of the Jews from Spain and Portugal in 1492, and another, smaller one following the rise of European fascism. At its height in the 1940s, Morocco's Jewish population numbered some 250,000 people. Growing up in Casablanca, [FIG. 3] which was then part of French-controlled Morocco,

FIG. 4 [PREVIOUS PAGE]
Morrocan fibula, 19th–early 20th century
Silver, enameled glass
Height: 46 7/16 inches (118 cm)
The Metropolitan Museum of Art; Gift of Marguerite McBey, 1981

FIG. 5 [ABOVE]
Carved Stars of David in the door of the Holy Ark in the
Neve Shalom Synagogue in Casablanca

El Hanani was immersed in French culture and language; both his parents attended the Alliance Israélite Universelle, which offered a French education to Jews throughout the Middle East, and his father, he recalls, "wanted to be more French than the French." His grandparents had closer ties with traditional Moroccan culture. Among the features of Moroccan life that impressed the artist was an ability to take time with daily tasks, an embrace of slowness that was visible in simple things such as how his grandparents made couscous by hand or carefully chopped ingredients for salads. El Hanani believes this attitude toward time, encapsulated by the popular Arabic phrase *shwaya shwaya* (slowly, slowly) may have influenced his work. Slowness or a sense of suspended time is also an aspect of Arabic music in which the concepts of *saltanah* and *tarab* (difficult to translate Arabic terms that refer to the ecstatic, trancelike aspects of traditional Arabic music) can involve the performer experiencing a sense of timelessness, as one can see in the famously lengthy performances of the Egyptian diva Umm Kalthoum. Certainly, it would be impossible to make work such as El Hanani's, which require many months of sustained attention, without possessing great patience, with a measure of *saltanah* and *tarab*.

It's not only in the domain of time that El Hanani's work reflects aspects of his North African origins. Interestingly, there are decorative motifs in Moroccan jewelry that closely resemble the modular units in some of El Hanani's drawings; more largely, the art made by Jews living in Arabic societies was permeated, as is Islamic art in general, with repetitive, non-representational forms that rely on slow accumulation. For instance, antique Berber jewelry from the Souss region of Southern Morocco sometimes employs a "wormhole" technique (especially for brooches or fibulae) in which many tiny silver cylinders are welded together, creating an effect suggestive of a piece of wood eaten away by worms. [FIG. 4 PAGE 13] Although worn by Berbers, wormhole fibulae were often made by Jewish silversmiths.[11] This is not to suggest

that El Hanani's "Circle" drawings were directly inspired by Berber jewelry, rather that the sensibility the artist brings to his drawings was formed, in part, by his exposure to the culture that could produce such objects. Arguably, the vast zone of Islamic, as well as Judeo-Islamic art, has exerted a significant influence on El Hanani's embrace of intricate patterning, both geometric and calligraphic, and on his process. He grew up in a Middle Eastern environment rich with densely designed, modular surfaces, whether found in the elaborately carved wooden doors of a Torah ark in a Casablanca synagogue or the simple tiled floors ubiquitous in Israeli homes. [FIG. 5]

As important as it might be to signal the role of Islamic and Judeo-Islamic forms of expression chez El Hanani, especially since this topic has been little discussed in writings on his work, a far greater influence is to be found in more expected sources: the New York avant-garde of the 1960s and 1970s, specifically Minimalism, Post-Minimalism, Conceptual Art and Performance Art. In other words, we must resist the temptation to exoticize El Hanani's work, while nonetheless acknowledging its unique provenance.

When El Hanani first arrived in New York in the early 1970s (he made an abortive attempt to establish himself in 1970 at the age of 23, and returned for good in 1974) [FIG.6 NEXT PAGE] he quickly realized that he had to eliminate all vestiges of representation from his work. Also purged were hierarchical compositions, what Donald Judd dismissively referred to as "relational painting." Finally able to see the canvases of the Abstract Expressionists and Color Field painters firsthand, and confronted with the recent work of artists such as Judd, Agnes Martin and, above all, Sol LeWitt, El Hanani began making allover works devoid of recognizable imagery. The work he had been making in Israel and France often depicted dense cityscapes in varying degrees of abstraction, in essence an École de Paris-derived style distinguished by sharp, economical lines.

FIG. 6 [BELOW]
Jacob El Hanani in his SoHo studio (where
he still works today), 1974

FIGS. 7A, B [OPPOSITE]
Installation views of the exhibition, *Black and White*, at
Galerie Denise René, New York, 1976. The group show included
work by Jacob El Hanani, Robert Indiana, Franz Kline,
Sol LeWitt, Marisol, Jesús Rafael Soto, and Victor Vasarely.

(In the 1960s, El Hanani supplemented his meager income by drawing political cartoons for Israeli newspapers—although his micrographic drawings couldn't be further in intention and appearance from such cartoons, arguably these two modes share a sureness of stroke and an economy of line. The artist continues to draw caricatures, which by now constitute a visual history of New York art world personalities, for his own amusement.) The impact of New York was all the more powerful because the dominant influence on Israeli art was European, while news about recent American art was hard to find.[12]

El Hanani has also noted the material "poverty" of the Israeli situation, and how that affected his practice, even after he moved to United States. As he explained in a 2016 video produced by The Metropolitan Museum of Art, "the tradition of colors or paint was not available for me, and paper was expensive in a country that has no trees."[13] Even in New York, paper was expensive, though certainly less so than the kinds of materials other artists were using, from traditional paint and canvas to the metal and Plexiglas favored by Minimalists or the more eccentric materials utilized by post-minimalist artists. If the choice of drawing with only ink (on paper and sometimes canvas) was dictated in part by El Hanani's specific financial situation, his commitment to drawing should also be seen as part of a wider development in which drawing was no longer seen as a secondary medium, something made on the way to a finished work, but could in the work of artists such as Sol LeWitt, Dorothea Rockburne, Hanne Darboven and Mel Bochner stand on its own as the center of a practice. [FIG. 8]

The influence of LeWitt on El Hanani is complicated. As Arthur Danto and others have pointed out, there are unmistakable similarities between El Hanani's and much of LeWitt's work, especially the latter's drawings of the late 1960s and 1970s. (There are also formal resemblances to the 1970s works of painters Brice Marden and Lucio Pozzi, whose compositional practice of dividing squares and rectangles was an influence that El Hanani readily acknowledges.) [FIG. 9 NEXT PAGE] It's not only the obvious visual echoes (allover linear patterns enclosed within square and rectangular boundaries), but also the philosophical underpinnings, the interest in systems and instructions: El Hanani appears to have taken to heart a number of passages from LeWitt's canonical text "Sentences on Conceptual Art," in particular #6 "If the artist changes his mind midway through the execution of the piece he compromises the result and repeats past results" and #7 "The artist's will is secondary to the process he initiates from idea to completion. His willfulness may only be ego." It could be argued that the artist was already primed for the anti-ego strictures of conceptual art thanks to the devotional discipline of Hebrew school where, as he has recalled, "turning a page 200 times a day became part of the way you grew up, repeating the same prayer."[14]

Yet El Hanani also rejected, consciously or not, some of LeWitt's central tenets, including the notion that anyone could make the work. In the 1970s LeWitt began hiring assistants to make his wall drawings, paying them by the hour; El Hanani, by contrast, even though he was influenced by the conceptual turn in art, could never outsource his work in this manner. The precision and stamina he brings to his

FIG. 8 [OPPOSITE]
Hanne Darboven
Untitled, 1974–75
Felt-tip pen on printed paper
16 $^1/_2$ x 11 $^3/_4$ inches (41.9 x 29.8 cm)
The Museum of Modern Art, New York; Partial gift of the Daled Collection and partial purchase through the generosity of Maja Oeri and Hans Bodenmann, Sue and Edgar Wachenheim III, Agnes Gund, Marlene Hess and James D. Zirin, Marie-Josée and Henry R. Kravis, and Jerry I. Speyer and Katherine G. Farley

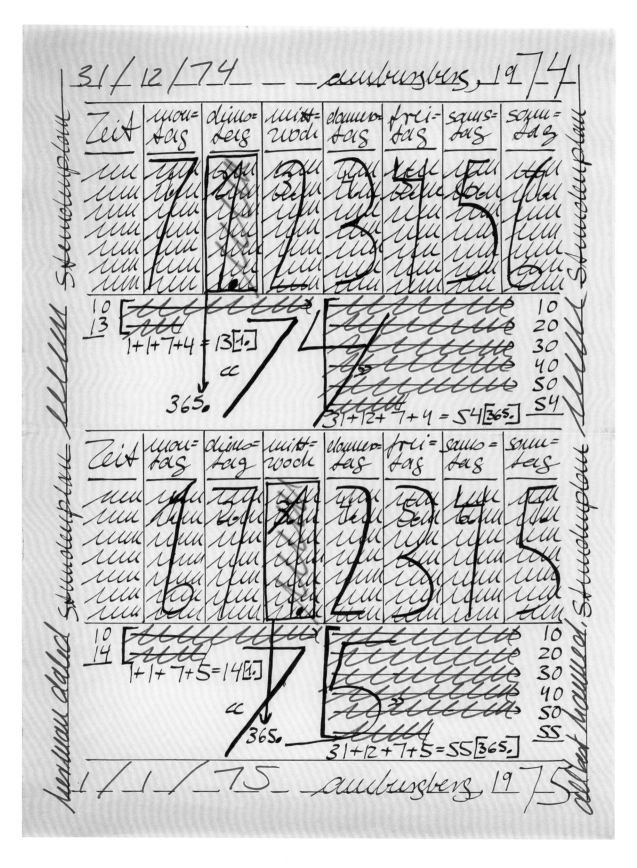

FIG. 9 [ABOVE]
Brice Marden
Grove IV, 1976
Oil and wax on canvas in two panels
72 x 108 inches (182.9 x 274.3 cm)
The Solomon R. Guggenheim Museum, New York; Purchased
with funds contributed by the National Endowment for the
Arts, in Washington D.C., a Federal agency; matching funds
contributed by Sidney Singer, 1976

FIG. 10 [OPPOSITE]
Maria Helena Vieira da Silva
The Corridor, 1950
Oil on canvas
25 $^1/_2$ x 35 $^7/_8$ inches (64.8 x 91 cm)
Tate; Purchased 1953

process are his alone; it's inconceivable that someone else could make these drawings. Because he shifted emphasis from the idea behind the work to its execution, El Hanani did not partake in the de-skilling that typified much conceptual art.[15] This might also be a good place to point out that by no means do all of El Hanani's drawings follow consistent procedures: there are many that follow an intuitive process or, as the artist explained to me, "lyrical movement versus austere movement." His recent "Turner" series, in which the accumulated marks create an atmospheric seascape, are examples of his "lyrical" side, as are other recent drawings that suggest the work of postwar lyrical abstractionist Maria Helena Vieira da Silva, whose heavily linear, textile-like paintings El Hanani knew well as a young man. [FIG. 10]

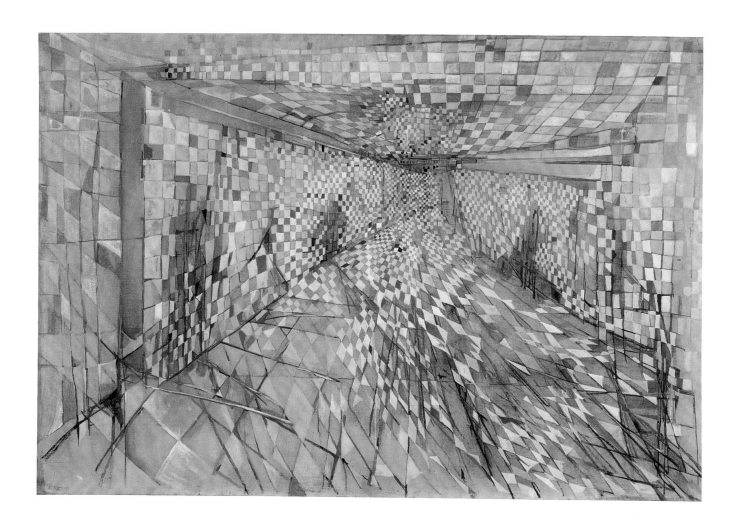

The work departs most profoundly from Minimalism in its ability to evoke specific contingencies in the world. Where Minimalism, and reductive art in general, sought to divest itself from specific references in order to achieve an autonomous content, El Hanani welcomes all sorts of allusions, whether they are made intentionally or emerge only after the fact, which is more often the case. Take, for instance, his series of "Gauze" drawings, exquisite nets of open-weave grids that seem to contract and expand like a breathing creature. Fabric, often drawn at 1-to-1scale, has long been a favored source for El Hanani, who derives inspiration from the challenge of translating three-dimensional textiles into line drawings. Of course, textiles, as artifacts of material culture, carry with them their deep histories, as turned out to be the case with the Gauze drawings. After having made a number of them it suddenly struck the artist that the etymology of "gauze" ultimately stretches back to the city of Gaza, which was a center of the weaving industry in the Middle Ages. Another after-the-fact association arose in the Hebrew Barbed Wire series, where sinuous lines are formed by the letters of the Hebrew alphabet. Only when looking at one of these completed drawings did El Hanani notice a resemblance to barbed wire, hence the title of the series. While the artist makes it clear that neither Gaza nor barbed wire were on his mind when he was making these drawings, he believes the associations may have existed at an unconscious level, that he may have been guided toward a barbed-wire motif not (as one might first think) because of association with the Shoah, but because barbed wire was ubiquitous in the Israel where he grew up in the 1950s. A different kind of associative process is at work in a set of drawings that rely on thousands of minute triangles. Having casually given them the name "Little Triangle Drawings," the artist was reminded of Israel's so-called Triangle, an area of land on the northern edge of the West Bank/Occupied Territories with a concentration of Arab towns and villages. (It's perhaps also worth noting that if two equilateral triangles are superimposed the result is the "Jewish" star.) Because of border location and its predominantly Arab population, the Triangle has figured in extremely controversial plans for an Israeli-Palestinian peace deal in which it would be ceded to the Palestinians in exchange for Israel taking land with Jewish settlement on the West Bank. El Hanani's drawings don't disclose his position on this proposed land swap, nor on Gaza, nor, indeed, on Israel-Palestinian relations at all. What they do accomplish however, especially once we become cognizant of their secondary allusions, is invite us to consider how humans ceaselessly territorialize; how any given territory is finite; how the closer together things/people become the more care must be given to their boundaries; how boundaries, like definitions of otherness, like the linked triangles in his drawings, are deeply interdependent. El Hanani is mapping not only his own daily existence, and the memories of his childhood, but also the possible future of any contested land.

Despite El Hanani's lack of interest in conceptual deskilling, there are interesting parallels between his approach and another mode of art that flourished in the 1970s: performance, in particular task-based works that required artists to repeat certain actions over extended periods of time. Although El Hanani has throughout his career been an unapologetic maker of objects, there is an aspect of his practice that relates to performance works such as Vito Acconci's early *Step Piece* (1970), which involved rapidly stepping off and on a stool to the point of exhaustion, to Tehching Hsieh's one-year performances such as *Cage Piece* (1978–79). As with such actions, the making of an El Hanani drawing is a feat of endurance, albeit broken up into roughly 15-minute sessions over a period of months or, sometimes, years. We might also cite the work of Roman Opalka, the painter who devoted his entire career to painting sequential numbers on one canvas after another. [FIG. 11] In all such works time plays an outsized role, and so, too, with El Hanani.

FIG. 11
Roman Opalka
1965 /1-∞, 1965
Acrylic on canvas
77 ¹/₄ x 53 ¹/₈ inches
(196 x 135 cm)
Private Collection

DETAIL

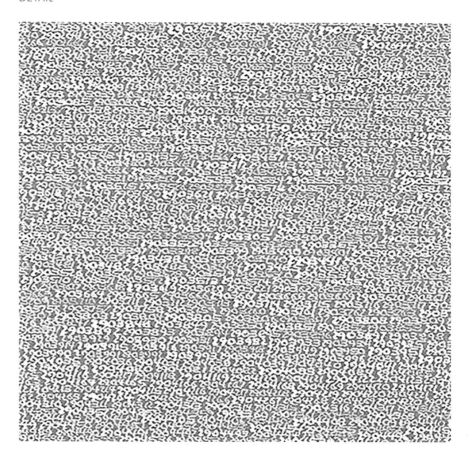

As he began making micrographic drawings, El Hanani understood that temporality, his relationship to time, would be crucial to his work, and also that he would experience it differently from most of the artists around him. First, it was clear that his drawings would take a lot of time to make; he wouldn't be able to create them by working only in the evenings or on weekends. Thus, he told himself, no day job, no teaching position, nothing that would take him out of his studio. In the beginning, and for many years to follow, he had little money but lots of time, and his work evolved in tandem with his economic situation. As he likes to say, he only spent seven dollars a year on materials (a bottle of ink and a few large sheets of paper, which at the time cost 50 cents a sheet). This set up a perfect equation: by spending very little on materials he guaranteed that he would have the time he needed to make his drawings, and the drawings themselves depended precisely on the thing he had in abundance: time. Plus, by crowding more and more marks onto a sheet of paper, he could further reduce his material costs. (The artist has told me of his subterfuge for acquiring free paper from Pearl Paint, the art-supply store on Canal Street frequented by SoHo artists: pretending to be shopping for paper, he would ask the person running the paper department for a sample of some high-quality paper. On another day when someone else was on duty he would return and again ask for a sample. In this way he was able to acquire paper for drawings, albeit very small ones.) From the beginning then, his art has been shaped by a strange contradiction between extreme frugality and an extravagant expenditure of time.

It occurs to me that another, and perhaps better, term than "time" for understanding El Hanani's work might be "duration." In the early 20th century, French philosopher Henri Bergson proposed the concept of duration (*la durée*) as a corrective to a positivist, mechanistic view of the world. By emphasizing the continuous nature of experience, presenting time not as something subject to measurement and division but as an unceasing, intuitively understood, memory-dependent process, Bergson sought to challenge the limitations of Western rationalism. One should always be careful when trying to equate the projects of philosophers and artists, but duration does seem to provide a useful way to think about El Hanani's art. These are not drawings that one can comprehend with a snapshot view; they require a commitment of time and attention simply to be seen, let alone understood. They insist on a unique protocol of viewing in which the usual strategies of positioning and time spent looking are useless. This is slow art at its purest, as slow in its making as in its viewing. But be forewarned, beneath this appearance of patience, beneath this modesty of means, beneath this partisanship with the diminutive lies a grand artistic ambition, a major achievement. As with the micro-writings of Benjamin and Walser, it is only with prolonged engagement that El Hanani's art offers up to us its concealed content, its single-minded intensity, and its intimate beauty.

ENDNOTES

1

Gershom Scholem, "Walter Benjamin," in Gershom Scholem, *On Jews and Judaism in Crisis: Selected Essays*, Schocken, New York, 1976, p. 177.

2

Quoted in *Walter Benjamin's Archive*, eds. Ursula Marx, Gudrun Schwarz, Michael Schwarz, Erdmut Wizisla, trans. Esther Leslie, Verso, London, New York, 2007, p. 50.

3

Scholem, p. 177.

4

Ibid.

5

It is only in the last decade with the publication of *Walter Benjamin's Archive* that Benjamin's hyper-condensed manuscripts and notes have become widely available. Interestingly, El Hanani, although he is familiar with Benjamin's writings, was not aware of the German's use of tiny script until quite recently, nor was the artist aware of Robert Walser's "microscripts," which are discussed later in this essay.

6

In 1965, Intel founder Gordon Moore predicted that the number of components that could be fitted into an integrated circuit would double every year. Interestingly, Moore's Law seems to be reaching the end of it life if only because of the limited economic benefits of chips measured in nanometers. The next step, already the focus of intensive research, is quantum computing, in which the computer becomes essentially invisible.

7

Susan Bernofsky, "Secrets, Not Code: On Robert Walser's *Microscripts*," in Robert Walser, *Microscripts*, New Directions/Christine Burgin, New York, 2012, p. 13.

8

Robert Walser, "Pencil Sketch," in Robert Walser, *Microscripts*, p. 31.

9

Bernofsky, p. 15.

10

Arthur Danto, "Small Wonders: The Art of Jacob El Hanani," in *Jacob El Hanani Drawings*, Acquavella Galleries, New York, 2015, p. 10.

11

See André Goldenberg, *Art and the Jews of Morocco*, Somogy, Paris, 2014. In his discussion of Moroccan broaches, Goldenberg emphasizes the intertwined nature of North African cultures. For instance, "The triangular shape of fibulae from the south, also found in other North African countries, can be classified among the polygonal shapes preferred by Jewish jewelers in the region, thus reflecting a Berber influence." p. 200.

12

Another Israeli artist of the same generation, Nahum Tevet, has described the European bias and cultural isolation of Israeli art at the time. See "Nahum Tevet in Conversation with Sarah Watson" in Thierry de Duve, *Nahum Tevet: Works on Glass, 1972-1975*, Hunter CUNY, New York, 2017.

13

Jacob El Hanani on the Mishneh Torah, The Metropolitan Museum of Art, The Artist Project, http://artistproject.metmuseum. org/6/jacob-el-hanani/. Accessed July 10, 2017.

14

Ibid.

15

El Hanani discusses his privileging of execution over idea in Isa Goldberg, "Making a Name for Himself," *Jerusalem Post*, March 1, 2010. http://www.jpost.com/Arts-and-Culture/ Arts/Making-a-name-for-himself. Accessed July 12, 2017.

NEXT PAGES
The Hebrew Mondrian, 2016
(DETAIL)

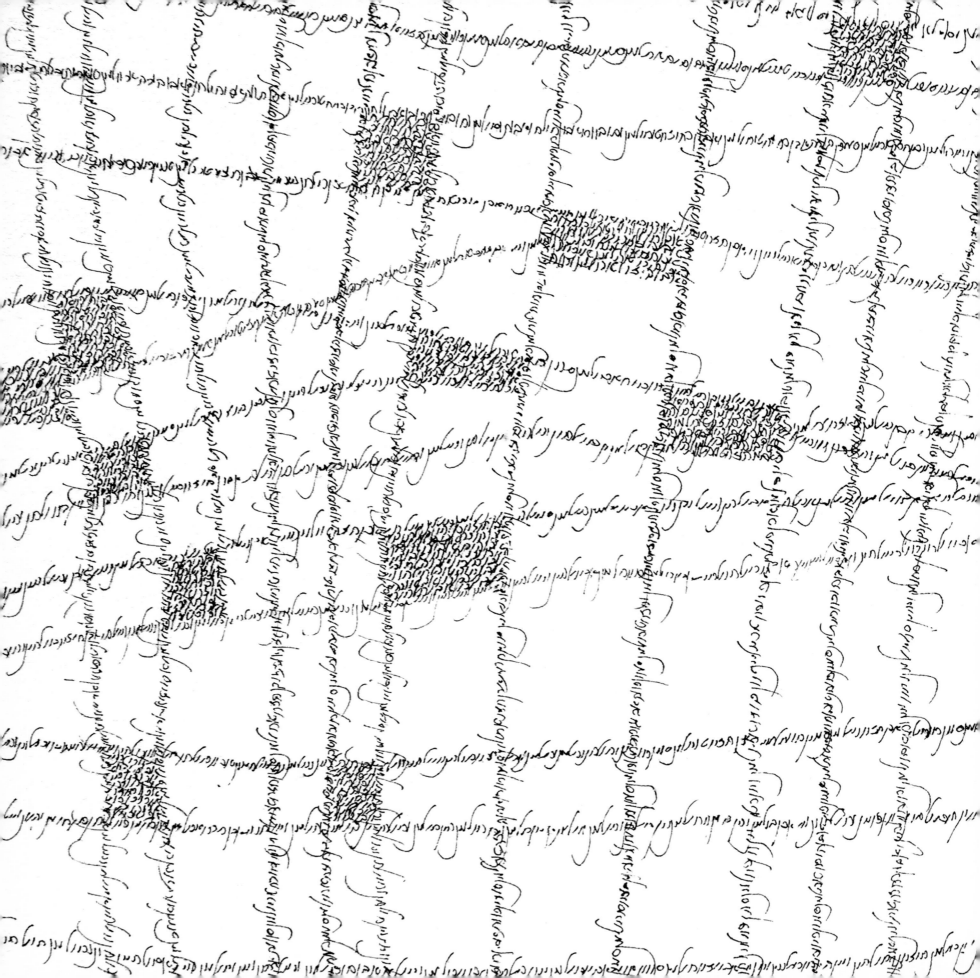

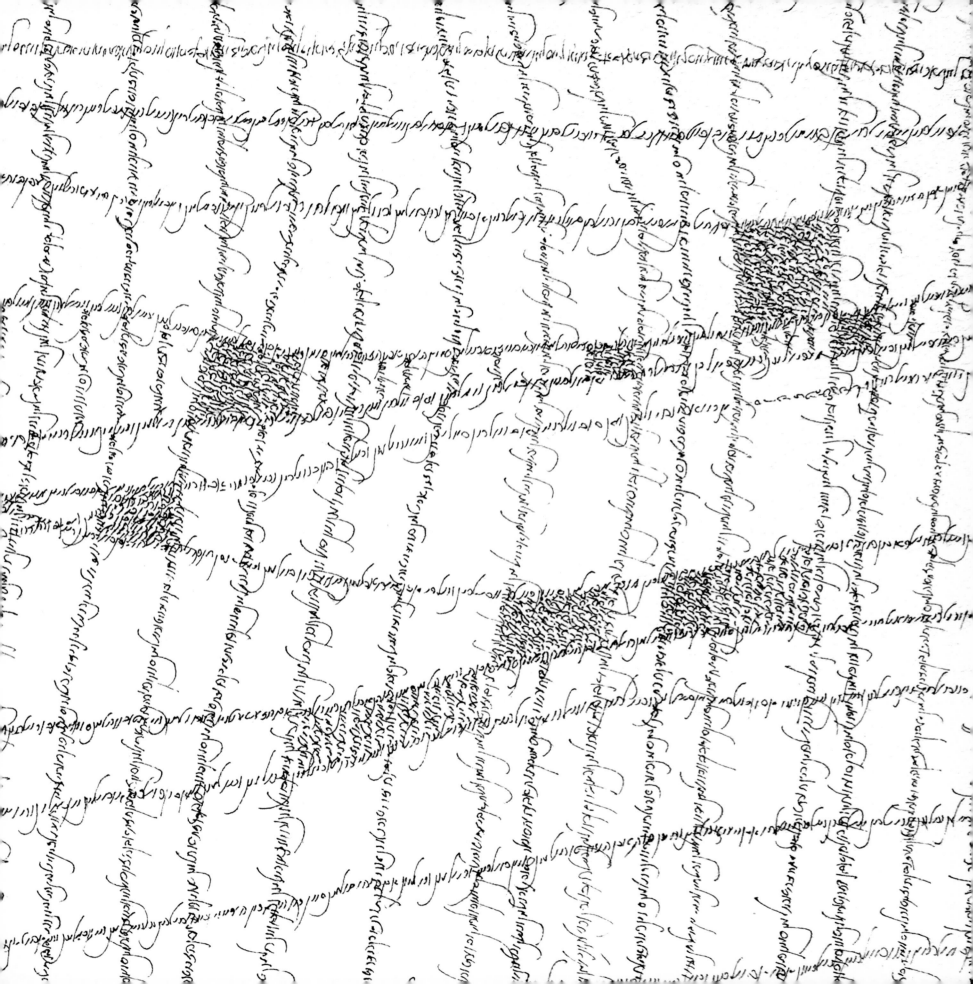

WORKS ON CANVAS

PLATE 1
Untitled 75, 1975
Ink on gessoed canvas
72 x 72 inches (182.9 x 182.9 cm)

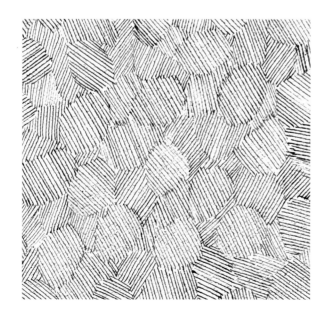

DETAIL (ACTUAL SIZE)

PLATE 2
Untitled 77, 1977
Ink on gessoed canvas
50 x 50 ¹/₄ inches (127 x 127.6 cm)

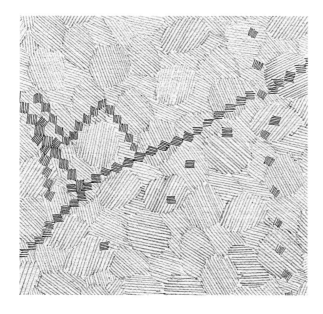

DETAIL (ACTUAL SIZE)

PLATE 3
Cubistic Linescape, 2016–17
Ink on gessoed canvas
50 1/8 x 50 1/8 inches (127.3 x 127.3 cm)

DETAIL (ACTUAL SIZE)

PLATE 4
NOF-Line, 2016 –17
Ink on gessoed canvas
50 x 50 inches (127 x 127 cm)

DETAIL (ACTUAL SIZE)

PLATE 5
Between Dot and Line, 2017
Ink on gessoed canvas
50 x 50 inches (127 x 127 cm)

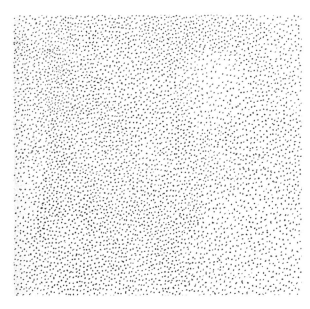

DETAIL (ACTUAL SIZE)

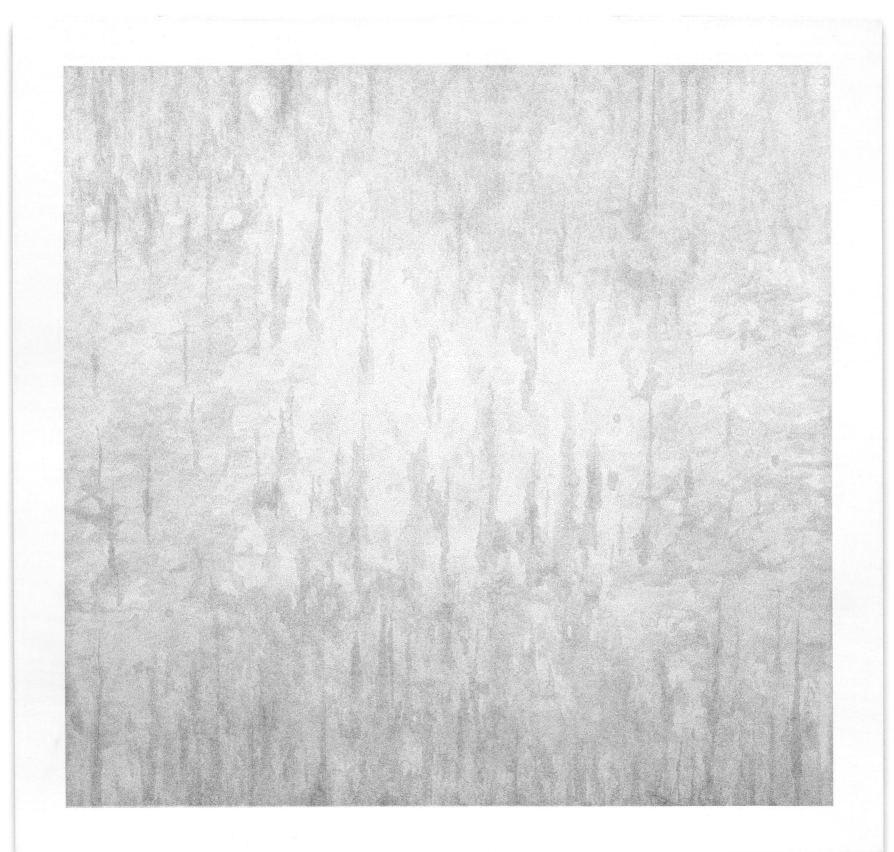

PLATE 6
Silver-Gray, 2015
Ink on gessoed canvas
22 $^{1}/_{8}$ x 22 inches (56.2 x 55.9 cm)

DETAIL (ACTUAL SIZE)

PLATE 7
Line by Line, 2015
Ink on gessoed canvas
22 $^{1}/_{8}$ x 22 inches (56.2 x 55.9 cm)

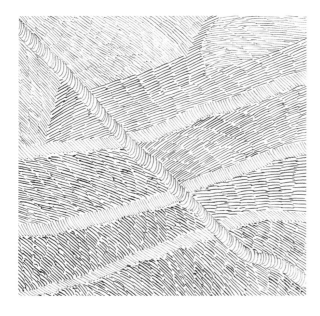

DETAIL (ACTUAL SIZE)

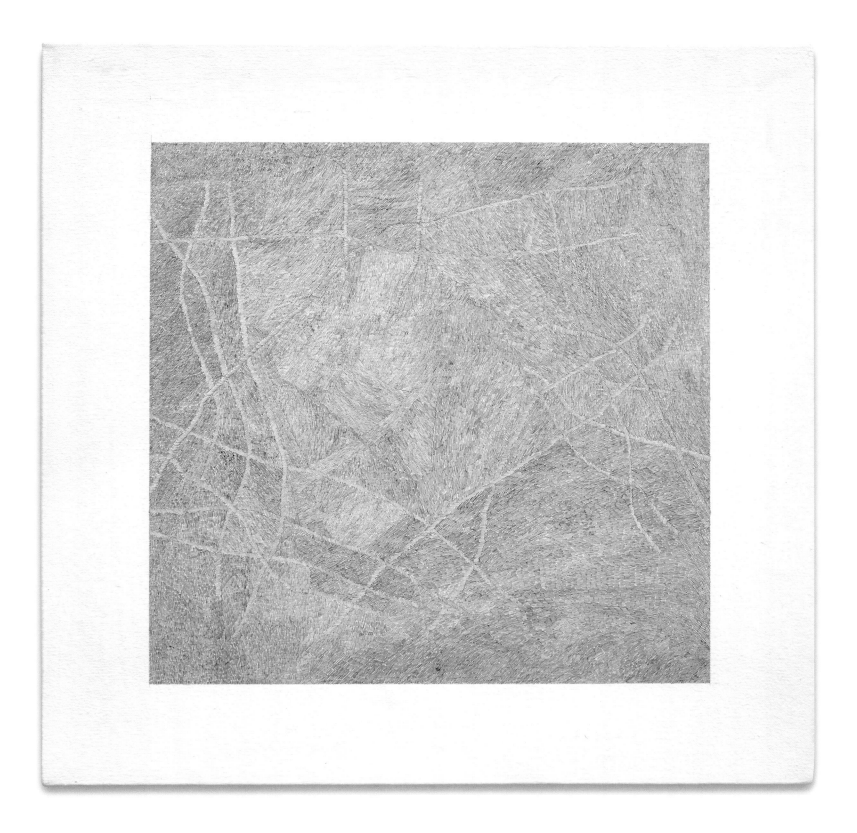

PLATE 8
White Square, 2016
Ink on gessoed canvas
15 $^{1}/_{8}$ x 15 $^{1}/_{8}$ inches (38.4 x 38.4 cm)

DETAIL (ACTUAL SIZE)

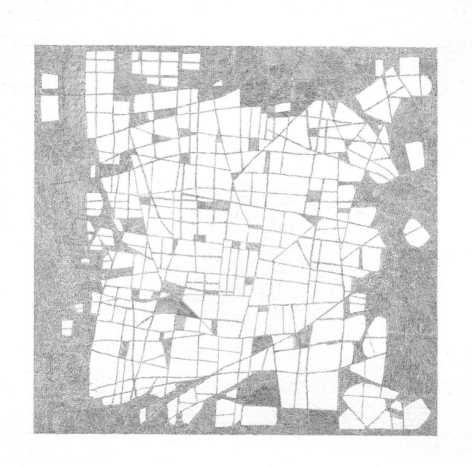

PLATE 9
Cross-Hatching Linescape, 2016
Ink on gessoed canvas
15 $^{1}/_{8}$ x 15 $^{1}/_{8}$ inches (38.4 x 38.4 cm)

DETAIL (ACTUAL SIZE)

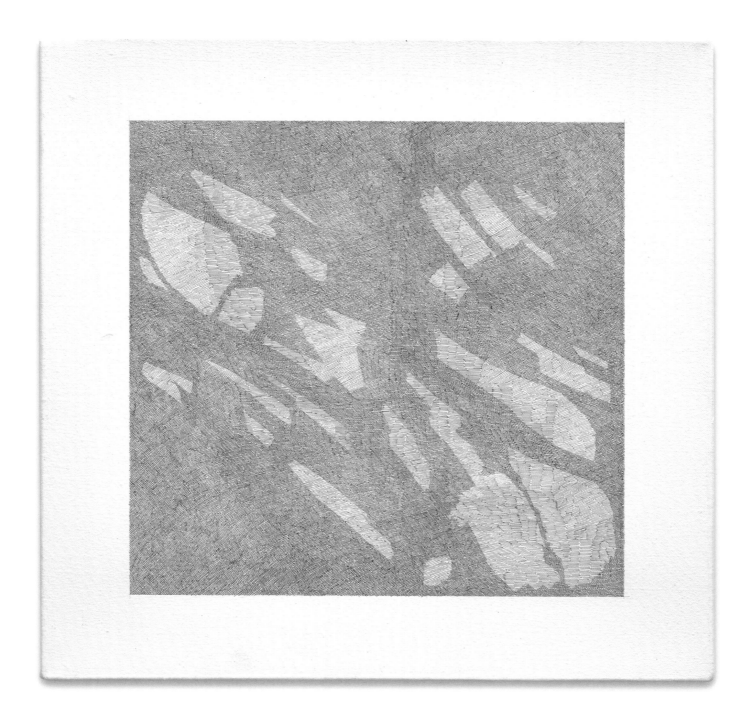

PLATE 10
Gray Skies, 2016
Ink on gessoed canvas
15 $^1/_8$ x 15 $^1/_8$ inches (38.4 x 38.4 cm)

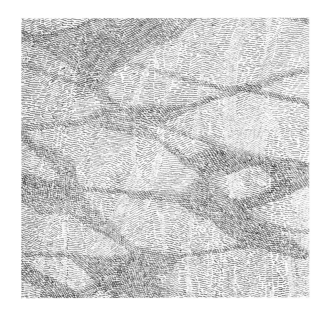

DETAIL (ACTUAL SIZE)

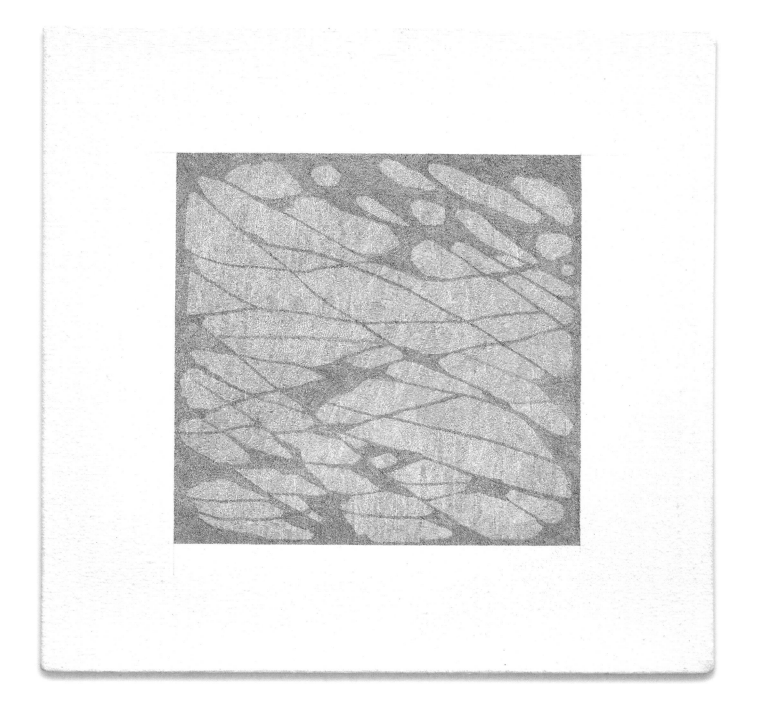

PLATE 11
Cloud Linescape, 2014
Ink on gessoed canvas
15 $^1/_8$ x 15 $^1/_4$ inches (38.4 x 38.7 cm)

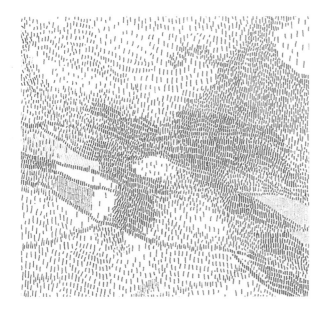

DETAIL (ACTUAL SIZE)

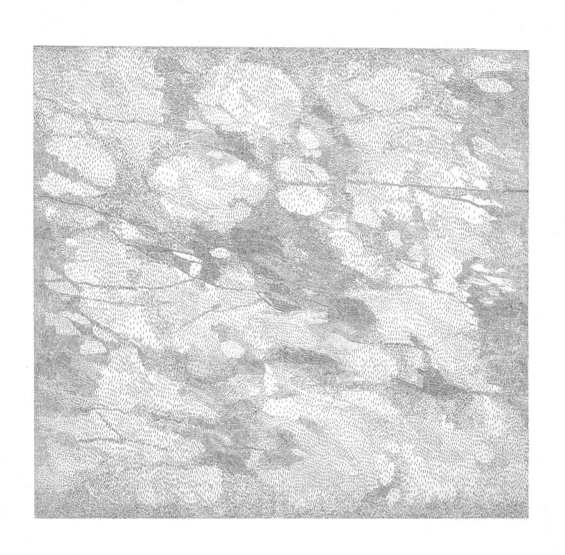

PLATE 12

The Hebrew Alphabet (from the Mondrian Series), 2016
Ink on gessoed canvas
15 ¹/₈ x 15 ¹/₈ inches (38.4 x 38.4 cm)

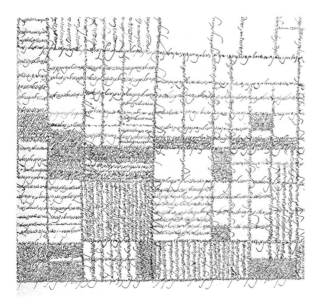

DETAIL (ACTUAL SIZE)

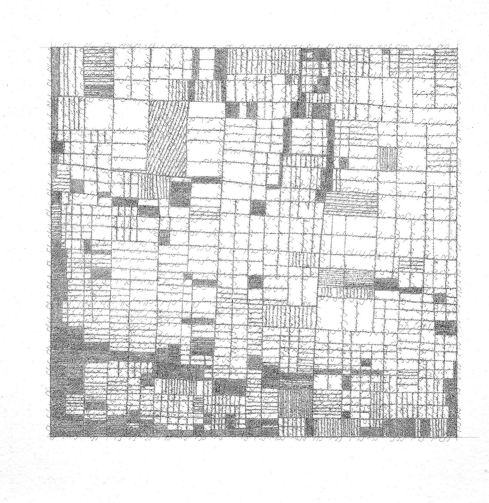

PLATE 13
NOF-Line, 2016
Ink on gessoed canvas
15 $\frac{1}{8}$ x 15 $\frac{1}{8}$ inches (38.4 x 38.4 cm)

DETAIL (ACTUAL SIZE)

WORKS ON PAPER

PLATE 14
Circle-NOF, 2006
Ink on paper
15 x 17 inches (38.1 x 43.2 cm)

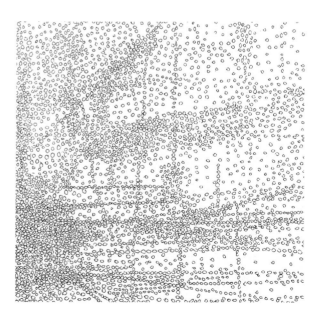

DETAIL (ACTUAL SIZE)

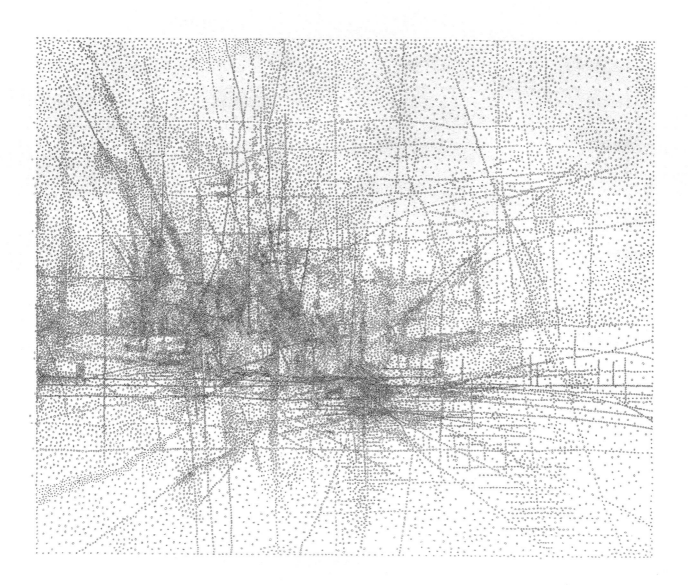

PLATE 15

Linear Scenery, 2004–05
Graphite on paper
15 x 20 inches (38.1 x 50.8 cm)

DETAIL (ACTUAL SIZE)

PLATE 16
Linescape (from the J. W. Turner Series), 2013
Ink on paper
14 $^1/_8$ x 20 $^1/_8$ inches (35.9 x 51.1 cm)

DETAIL (ACTUAL SIZE)

PLATE 17
Untitled 78, 1978
Ink on paper
16 x 19 inches (40.6 x 48.3 cm)

DETAIL (ACTUAL SIZE)

PLATE 18
Partition, 2007
Ink on paper
18 ¹/₈ x 24 inches (46 x 61 cm)

DETAIL (ACTUAL SIZE)

PLATE 19
Vertical=Horizontal, 2007–17
Ink on paper
18 $\frac{1}{8}$ x 24 inches (46 x 61 cm)

DETAIL (ACTUAL SIZE)

PLATE 20
Circles 08, 2008
Ink on paper
18 $^1/_8$ x 23 $^7/_8$ inches (46 x 60.6 cm)

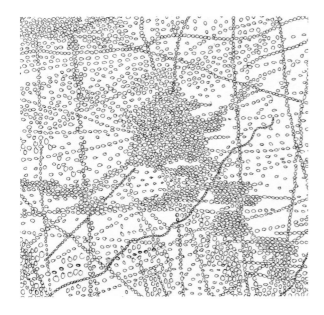

DETAIL (ACTUAL SIZE)

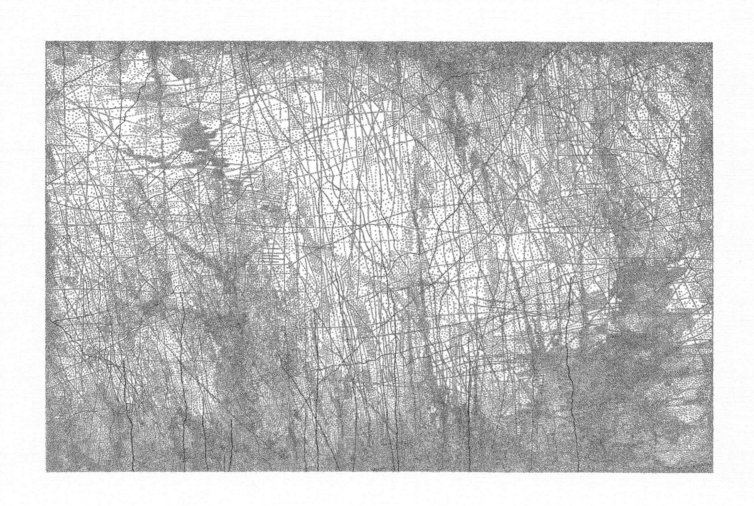

PLATE 21
Urban Landscape (from the Linear Landscape Series), 2010
Ink on paper
18 x 18 inches (45.7 x 45.7 cm)

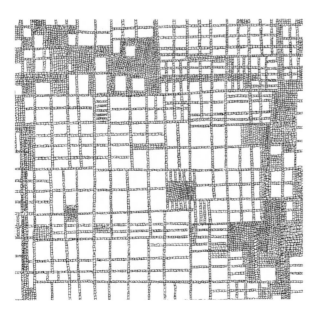

DETAIL (ACTUAL SIZE)

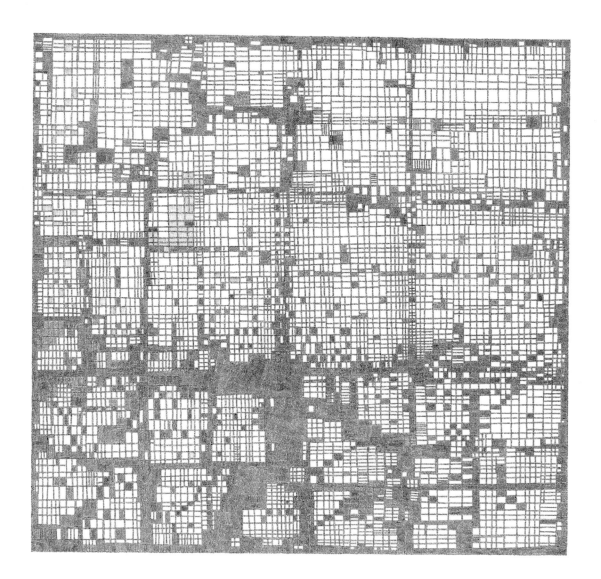

PLATE 22
Gevaot (Hill), 1980
Ink on paper
16 x 17 $^{5}/_{8}$ inches (40.6 x 44.8 cm)

DETAIL (ACTUAL SIZE)

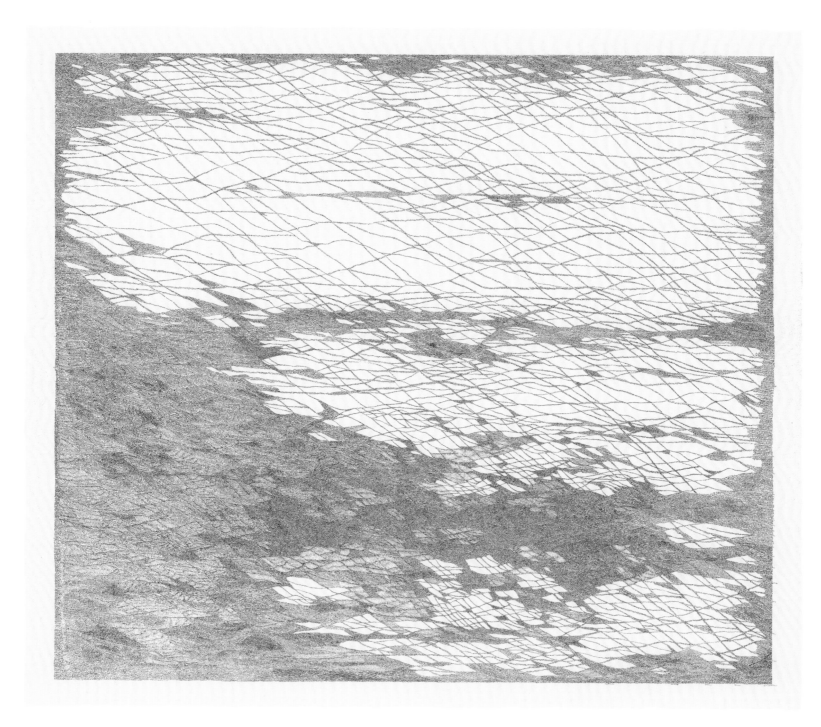

PLATE 23
Quadric Surface, 2003
Ink on paper
18 $^1/_8$ x 18 $^1/_8$ inches (46 x 46 cm)

DETAIL (ACTUAL SIZE)

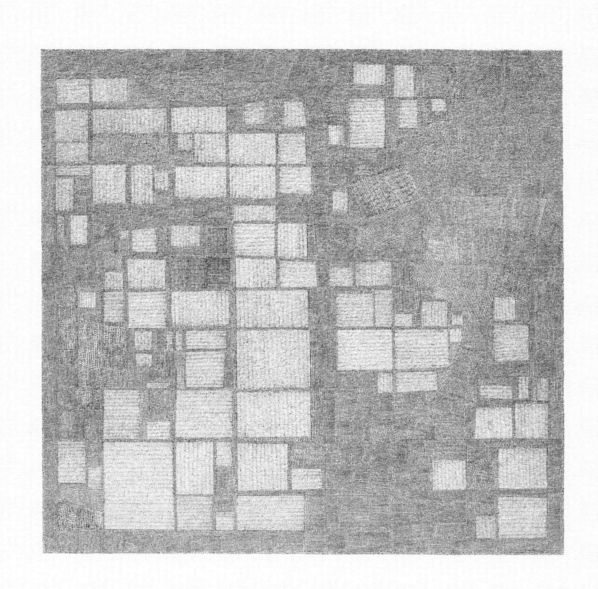

PLATE 24
Untitled (from the Mondrian Series), 2011
Ink on paper
18 x 18 inches (45.7 x 45.7 cm)

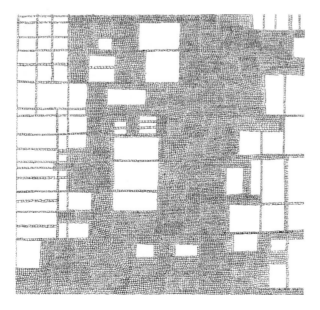

DETAIL (ACTUAL SIZE)

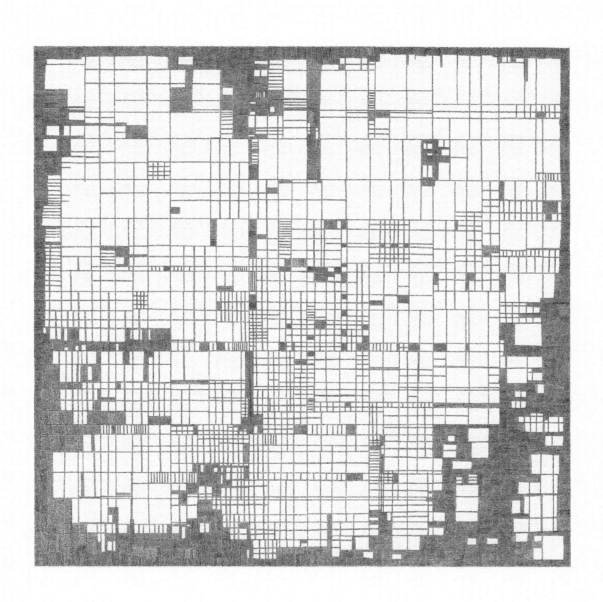

PLATE 25
Linescape (from the J. W. Turner Series), 2014–15
Ink on paper
26 x 40 inches (66 x 101.6 cm)

DETAIL (ACTUAL SIZE)

PLATE 26
Linescape (from the J. W. Turner Series), 2012
Ink on paper
22 x 28 inches (55.9 x 71.1 cm)

DETAIL (ACTUAL SIZE)

PLATE 27
Linescape (from the J. W. Turner Series), 2015–16
Ink on paper
29 ¹/₈ x 39 ⁷/₈ inches (74 x 101.3 cm)

DETAIL (ACTUAL SIZE)

PLATE 28
The Hebrew Barbed Wire, 2012
Ink on paper
12 x 12 inches (30.5 x 30.5 cm)

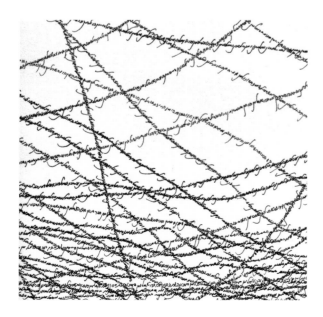

DETAIL (ACTUAL SIZE)

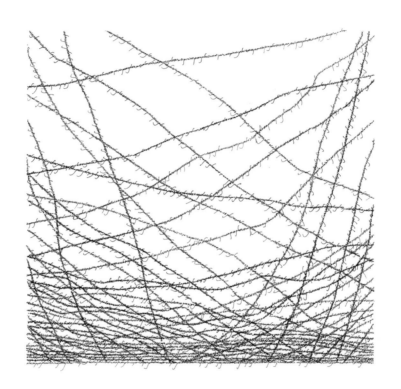

PLATE 29
Lavender Gauze, 2015
Ink on paper
19 x 25 $^1/_8$ inches (48.3 x 63.8 cm)

DETAIL (ACTUAL SIZE)

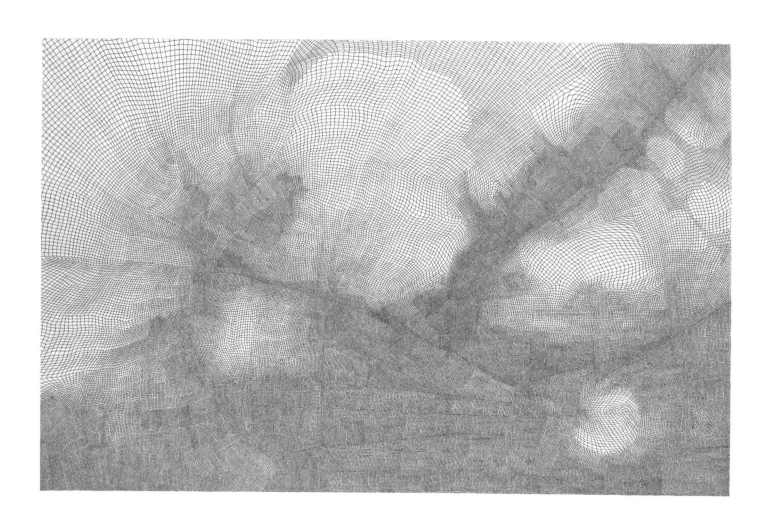

PLATE 30
Gray Gauze, 2016
Ink on paper
25 $^{7}/_{8}$ x 26 inches (65.7 x 66 cm)

DETAIL (ACTUAL SIZE)

PLATE 31
Alhambra, 2016
Ink on paper
25 $^7/_8$ x 25 $^3/_4$ inches (65.7 x 65.4 cm)

DETAIL (ACTUAL SIZE)

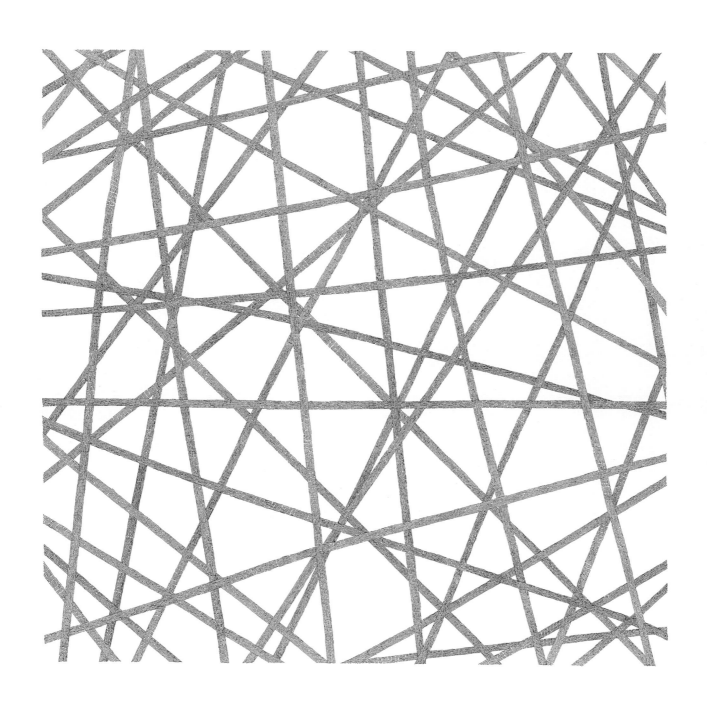

PLATE 32
The Hebrew Mondrian, 2016
Ink on paper
26 $^{1}/_{4}$ x 26 inches (66.7 x 66 cm)

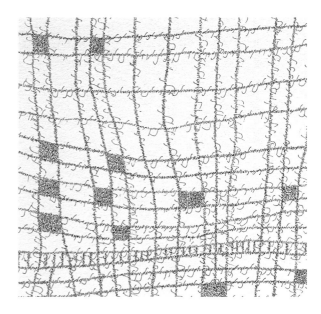

DETAIL (ACTUAL SIZE)

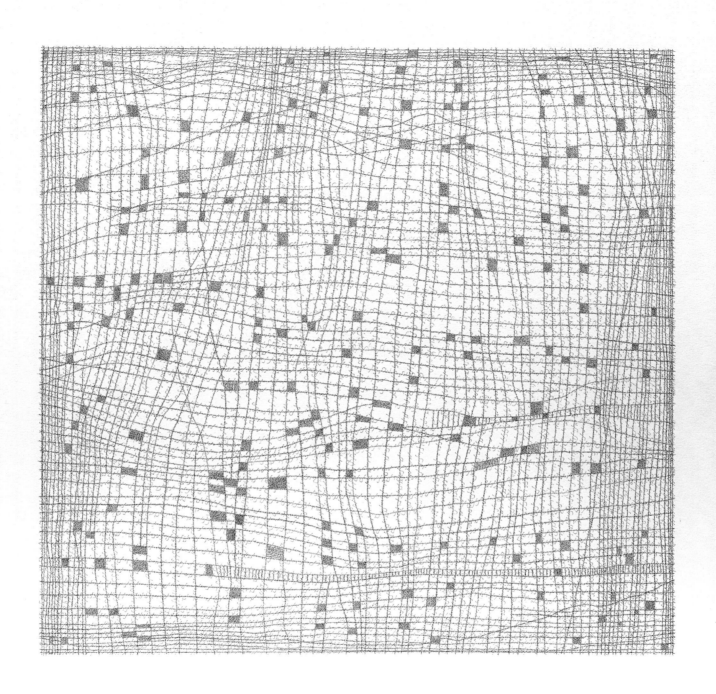

PLATE 33
Cursive Hebrew Alphabet, 2006
Ink on paper
6 x 9 inches (15 x 23 cm)

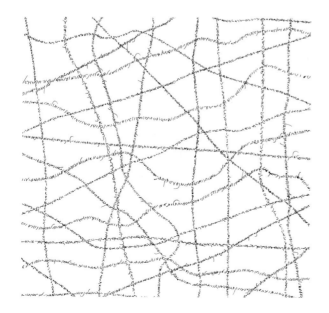

DETAIL (ACTUAL SIZE)

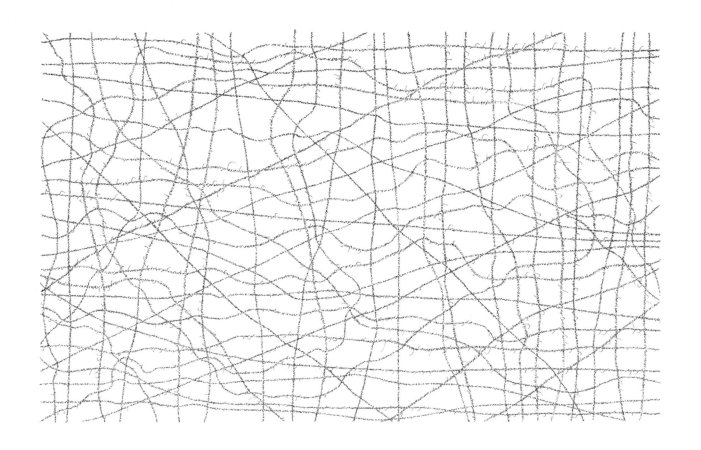

JACOB EL HANANI

1947   Born Casablanca, Morocco

Education

1969   Avni School of Fine Arts, Tel Aviv, Israel

1970   École des Beaux-Arts, Paris, France

Solo Exhibitions

2017   *Jacob EL Hanani Linescape: Four Decades*, Acquavella
Galleries, New York, NY

2015   *Jacob El Hanani: Drawings*, Acquavella Galleries,
New York, NY

2014   *The Art of the Line*, Sammer Gallery LLC, Miami, FL

2012   *Linear Landscape: Ink Drawings*, Holly Johnson Gallery,
Dallas, TX

2008   *Recent Work*, Steven Zevitas Gallery, Boston, MA

2005   *Drawing 1978–2005*, Mills College, Oakland, CA

2004   *Jacob El Hanani Drawings 1971–1987*,
Gallery Schlesinger, New York, NY

2003   OSP Gallery, Boston, MA

2002   Nicole Klagsbrun Gallery, New York, NY
Gallery Joe, Philadelphia, PA

2000   Mark Moore Gallery, Santa Monica, CA
Nicole Klagsbrun Gallery, New York, NY
Gallery Joe, Philadelphia, PA

1999   Miller/Block Gallery, Boston, MA

1998   Todd Hosfelt Gallery, San Francisco, CA

1995   Yoshii Gallery, New York, NY

1993   Galerie Renee Ziegler, Zurich

1988   Galerie Gilbert Brownstone, Paris

1978   Galerie Denise René, Paris

1977   Galerie Denise René, New York, NY

1975   Galerie Denise René, Paris

Selected Museum Collections (in order of acquisition)

The Solomon R. Guggenheim Museum, New York

The Museum of Modern Art, New York

The Jewish Museum, New York

The Brooklyn Museum, New York

Musée National d'Art Moderne, Centre Georges Pompidou, Paris

The Israel Museum, Jerusalem

Art Gallery of Ontario, Toronto

The Menil Collection, Houston

The Metropolitan Museum of Art, New York

The Philadelphia Museum of Art

The Hirshhorn Museum and Sculpture Garden, Smithsonian
Institution, Washington, D.C.

The Art Institute of Chicago

Walker Art Center, Minneapolis

The Tel-Aviv Museum of Art, Israel

The National Gallery of Art, Washington

Museo de Arte Contemporáneo de Caracas, Venezuela

The Rose Art Museum, Brandeis University, Waltham, MA

Minneapolis Institute of Arts, MN

Yale University Art Gallery, New Haven, CT

The Museum of Fine Arts, Houston

The Museum of Fine Arts, Boston

The Fogg Art Museum, Harvard University Art Museums, Cambridge, MA

Weatherspoon Art Museum, University of North Carolina at Greensboro, NC

Neuberger Museum of Art, Purchase College State University of New York

The British Museum, London

The Whitney Museum of American Art, New York

The Morgan Library & Museum, New York

Pérez Art Museum Miami

Linescape (from the J. W. Turner Series), 2012 (DETAIL)

PHOTO CREDITS

Unless otherwise noted, all photos by Kent Pell.

Page 10: Reproduced in Walter Benjamin's Archive, Verso, 2007, page 70. WBA Ms 502. **Page 11**: By Robert Walter, translated by Susan Bernofsky, from The Microscripts. Copyright © Suhrkamp Verlag Zurich and Frankfurt am Main 1985. Reprinted by permission of New Directions Publishing Corp. **Page 12**: Photo courtesy Zvi Elhyani. **Page 13**: Image copyright © The Metropolitan Museum of Art. Image source: Art Resource, NY. **Page 14**: Photo: Richard Nowitz / Getty Images: National Geographic Collection. **Pages 16–17**: Photos courtesy Jacob El Hanani. **Page 19**: Digital Image © The Museum of Modern Art / Licensed by SCALA / Art Resource, NY. Art © 2017 Artists Rights Society (ARS), New York / VG Bild-Kunst, Bonn. **Page 20**: Image © The Solomon R. Guggenheim Foundation / Art Resource, NY. Art © 2017 Brice Marden / Artists Rights Society (ARS), New York. **Page 21**: © Tate, London / Art Resource, NY. Art © 2017 Artists Rights Society (ARS), New York / ADAGP, Paris. **Page 23**: Photo © Christie's Images / Bridgeman Images. Art © 2017 Artists Rights Society (ARS), New York / ADAGP, Paris.